Forest Birds of the West

MW01140507

Genevieve Einstein
& Einstein Sisters

KidsWorld

Quick Guide

These are some of the birds that you are most likely to see in forests of Western North America. We've included their measurements in case you want to have fun with rulers!

Wood Duck p. 8
Length: 20 in (50 cm)

Mallard p. 10
Length: 22 in (57 cm)

Hooded Merganser p. 12
Length: 18 in (45 cm)

Wild Turkey p. 14
Length: 44 in (112 cm)

Ruffed Grouse p. 16
Length: 18 in (45 cm)

Mourning Dove p. 18
Length: 11 in (28 cm)

Common Nighthawk p. 20
Length: 9 in (23 cm)

Black-chinned Hummingbird p. 22
Length: 4 in (10 cm)

Spotted Sandpiper p. 24
Length: 7 in (18 cm)

Ring-billed Gull p. 26
Length: 19 in (48 cm)

Turkey Vulture p. 28
Length: 29 in (73 cm)

Cooper's Hawk p. 30
Length: 16 in (41 cm)

Northern Goshawk p. 32
Length: 23 in (59 cm)

Bald Eagle p. 34
Length: 33 in (84 cm)

Western Screech-Owl p. 36
Length: 9 in (23 cm)

Spotted Owl p. 38
Length: 19 in (48 cm)

Long-eared Owl p. 40
Length: 15 in (38 cm)

Northern Saw-whet Owl p. 42
Length: 8 in (20 cm)

Lewis's Woodpecker p. 44
Length: 11 in (28 cm)

Hairy Woodpecker p. 46
Length: 9 in (23 cm)

Pileated Woodpecker p. 48
Length: 18 in (45 cm)

Merlin p. 50
Length: 11 in (28 cm)

Steller's Jay p. 52
Length: 13 in (32 cm)

Common Raven p. 54
Length: 25 in (63 cm)

Violet-green Swallow p. 56
Length: 5 in (12 cm)

Chestnut-backed Chickadee p. 58
Length: 4 in (10 cm)

Bushtit p. 60
Length: 3 in (8 cm)

White-breasted Nuthatch p. 62
Length: 6 in (14 cm)

Brown Creeper p. 64
Length: 5 in (12 cm)

House Wren p. 66
Length: 5 in (12 cm)

Blue-gray Gnatcatcher p. 68
Length: 4 in (10 cm)

Golden-crowned Kinglet p. 70
Length: 4 in (10 cm)

Western Bluebird p. 72
Length: 7 in (18 cm)

Swainson's Thrush p. 74
Length: 7 in (18 cm)

Gray Catbird p. 76
Length: 9 in (23 cm)

Cedar Waxwing p. 78
Length: 6 in (14 cm)

Red Crossbill p. 80
Length: 7 in (18 cm)

Pine Siskin p. 82
Length: 5 in (12 cm)

Chipping Sparrow p. 84
Length: 6 in (14 cm)

Song Sparrow p. 86
Length: 6 in (14 cm)

Bullock's Oriole p. 88
Length: 7 in (18 cm)

Yellow-rumped Warbler p. 90
Length: 5 in (12 cm)

Western Tanager p. 92
Length: 7 in (18 cm)

Black-headed Grosbeak p. 94
Length: 7 in (18 cm)

How to Use this Book

Each bird in this book has icons in the right-hand corner. These icons quickly tell you the size of the bird, where to look for it, what food it eats and what kind of nest it builds.

Size

Small is for birds that are shorter than the length of a school ruler (1 ft/30 cm).

Medium is for birds that are between one and two school rulers long (1-2 ft/30-60 cm).

Large is for birds that are bigger than two school rulers placed end to end (2 ft/60 cm).

Where to Look

On or close to the ground.

On or close to the water.

In trees or shrubs.

In the air.

Food

 Seeds, flowers or other plant parts.

 Fruits or berries.

 Insects or other creepy crawlies.

 Fish or other water animals.

 Land animals (like mice) or birds.

Nests

Simple nests are often on the ground. Birds don't put much effort into simple nests.

Cup-shaped nests are often found in trees. These are usually made with vegetation.

Some birds like to nest in tree cavities or nest boxes.

Some birds have nests that are unusual. They don't fit into the other categories.

Wood Duck

Wood Ducks have claws on their webbed feet! The claws at the tips of their toes help them grip onto tree branches.

Q: Where do the royal birds live?
A: At Duckingham Palace!

A Wood Duck can lay as many as 20 eggs in one nest. That's a lot of brothers and sisters!

The Wood Duck nests in a tree cavity. Some nests can be as high in the tree as the top of a 4-storey building. Because they can't fly yet, nestlings have to jump out of the nest and fall to the ground or water below!

One nickname for the Wood Duck is squealer because of the male's squeaky *jeeb* call.

Male ducks are called drakes. Many drakes have colorful feathers to impress the plainer-looking females, called hens.

9

Mallard

Most ducks don't actually quack. The female Mallard is one of the only ducks that makes a quacking sound.

Mallards tip up in the water with their bums in the air to eat plants or bugs below the surface.

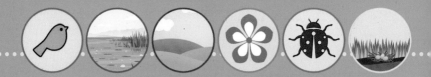

A female Mallard plucks feathers from her breast and belly to line her nest. When she incubates her eggs, the bare patch on her underside helps keep the eggs warm.

For the first two weeks after they hatch, Mallard chicks huddle together to stay warm.

Ducks shed their flight feathers once a year to grow new ones. For about one month in the summer while its new flight feathers are growing in, this bird can't fly!

11

Hooded Merganser

The Hooded Merganser's feet are far back on its body. This helps the duck swim underwater, but it makes it hard to walk on land.

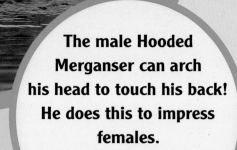

The male Hooded Merganser can arch his head to touch his back! He does this to impress females.

Mergansers are nicknamed sawbills because of the tooth-like texture on their bills. The jagged edges help this bird catch and handle the fish it eats.

Other species of cavity nesting ducks sometimes lay their eggs in this bird's nest. The most eggs found in a Hooded Merganser nest is 44!

13

Wild Turkey

The Wild Turkey can run faster than you! It can run about as fast as an Olympic sprinter.

This bird's bald head can change color to pink, blue or white depending on its mood!

A group of turkeys can be called a gang, a posse or a raffle.

In spring the male walks around with his tail fanned and his wings dragging on the ground to impress females.

Q: Why did the turkey cross the road twice? A: To prove he wasn't chicken!

The Wild Turkey almost went extinct in the 1930s because of overhunting and loss of forests. Thankfully these interesting birds are now common again!

15

Ruffed Grouse

The Ruffed Grouse's plumage closely matches the color of the forest floor, helping the bird hide from predators.

The Ruffed Grouse finds most of its food on the ground. It will sometimes fly into trees to eat fruit or escape danger.

The male makes a drumming sound with his wings. When drumming, he beats his wings up to 5 times per second!

In the fall, this bird develops extra scales on its toes. These scales make the toes wider and work like snowshoes in deep snow.

17

Mourning Dove

The Mourning Dove is considered the official symbol of peace in some U.S. states.

This dove can continue to eat even after its stomach is full! It has a storage pouch in its throat, called a crop, that stores the extra food.

When this dove flies, its wings make a whistling sound. The sound is easiest to hear when a group of doves fly together.

When the female Mourning Dove builds her nest, the male passes her twigs or stems while standing on her back!

Once young birds leave the nest, they have two weeks to learn how to find food with the help of the male. After that, they are on their own.

Common Nighthawk

The **Common Nighthawk** can be found in forest clearings and along forest edges. You are most likely to see it flying like a bat at dusk and dawn, sometimes in a big group called a **kettle**.

Often called a **mosquito hawk**, this bird eats flying insects that it catches while in flight. It can eat as many as 500 mosquitoes in one day!

The Common Nighthawk lays its eggs on the ground without building a nest.

If her eggs are threatened, the female may perform a distraction display, pretending to be injured. She may also lunge at the predator.

Black-chinned Hummingbird

The female Black-chinned Hummingbird feeds her chicks by sticking her long bill into theirs and vomiting up insects and nectar.

The female works hard making her tiny, apricot-sized nest. The nest is made mostly out of plant down and spider web silk. It is stretchy and expands as the chicks grow.

When it is cold outside, this little bird can drink up to three times its weight in nectar! It can survive without nectar if it has lots of insects to eat.

The Black-chinned Hummingbird has two grooves on its tongue that help it drink nectar. When feeding it licks up to 17 times per second!

Spotted Sandpiper

The Spotted Sandpiper's body bobs up and down when it stands or walks. This behavior has earned it many nicknames, including teeter-peep.

Q: What do birds wear to the beach?
A: Beak-inis!

This sandpiper eats mostly insects and other small creatures that it finds on beaches or in the water. It catches them with a quick jabbing motion of its long bill.

This sandpiper has spots on its breast only in summer. The spots help camouflage the bird on pebbled beaches.

The male Spotted Sandpiper spends more time incubating eggs than the female does. Chicks can walk around and feed themselves within a few hours of hatching!

25

Ring-billed Gull

Like most gulls, the Ring-billed Gull isn't a picky eater. Its favorite food is fish, but it also eats insects, grain, mice and even garbage!

This bird often nests on small, forested islands within flying range of towns or cities.

This gull nests in large colonies. Members of a colony communicate with loud *kakaka* and *keeaah* calls. Colonies can be so loud that people working near them may need to wear ear protection to prevent hearing damage!

Adult birds have a black stripe on a yellow bill.

In spring and summer this gull's head is white, but in fall and winter its head is a mix of white and gray.

27

Turkey Vulture

The **Turkey Vulture** eats the flesh of dead animals. Its strong sense of smell helps it find carcasses it can't see.

This bird has no feathers on its head so that bits of food won't get stuck in them. The vulture feeds on messy carcasses.

The Turkey Vulture can survive for up to two weeks without food. It will eat poop if it gets really hungry!

As young as one week old, nestlings can defend themselves against predators by throwing up on the intruders!

This funny-looking bird has the odd habit of perching in a tree with its wings stretched out. It likely does this to warm up, cool off or dry off.

29

Cooper's Hawk

Female and male Cooper's Hawks look similar, but the male is smaller than the female. The male also has a higher pitched voice.

The Cooper's Hawk uses its strong talons catch and kill its prey.

The Cooper's Hawk flies quickly through thick forests to catch small birds or rodents. This isn't easy to do, and many hawks are injured and break bones during their lives!

The male helps build the nest. When the eggs hatch, he takes food to the female, and she feeds it to the nestlings.

Young Cooper's Hawks are brown and white.

Q: What is a hawk's favorite sport? A: Hawkey!

Northern Goshawk

For more than 2000 years, people have trained **Northern Goshawks** to hunt for them. These birds earned the nickname **cook's hawk** because they are so good at catching a meal.

When chasing its prey, the Northern Goshawk doesn't give up. It will crash through bushes or enter water to catch a bird or rodent.

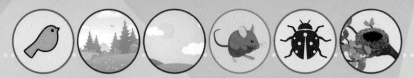

The Northern Goshawk's short, strong wings allow it to speed up quickly when flying. Its long tail helps it change direction easily when flying through trees.

The female often adds fresh conifer sprigs to the nest. Chemicals in the conifer needles may help keep insects and fungus out of the nest.

33

Bald Eagle

The Bald Eagle is the second largest bird of prey in North America, after the California Condor.

It gets its white head at 5½ years old. Until then, its head is mostly brown.

The Bald Eagle eats many different foods, including rodents, reptiles, crustaceans and birds. Its favorite food is fish.

This eagle is a great hunter, but it prefers to steal food. It often swipes fish from Ospreys or other eagles. It will also rob mammals, like sea otters and foxes of their catch.

This bird builds a big nest at the top of a tree. The largest Bald Eagle nest ever recorded was as wide as 5 school desks placed side by side and about as tall as a 2-storey building!

Western Screech-Owl

The Western Screech-Owl's camouflage is so good that it can hardly be seen against the bark of the trees where it perches.

Q: Why do owls always get invited to bird parties?
A: Because they're such a hoot!

This little owl is a great nighttime hunter. It can catch prey much bigger than itself, including rabbits! It also eats insects, worms, small birds and rodents.

This owl is small enough to use tree cavities for nesting. The young are good climbers and learn to fly when they are about one month old.

Spotted Owl

The Spotted Owl lives in forests with trees that are at least 150 years old. This owl is less common than it used to be. It has lost much of its habitat because the trees were cut down for timber.

The Spotted Owl eats flying squirrels, rats and rabbits. It eats its prey whole. Whatever its stomach can't digest (bones, fur and teeth) it spits out as a pellet.

Owl Pellet

Most owls have yellow or red eyes, but the Spotted Owl has dark eyes that often appear black.

A group of owls is called a wisdom or a parliament of owls.

Owlets don't have spots until they get their adult feathers.

Long-eared Owl

The Long-eared Owl's ear tufts look like ears, but these feather tufts have nothing to do with the owl's hearing.

Outside of the nesting season, these owls sometimes gather in groups of up to 100 birds to sleep in trees.

The Long-eared Owl is a nighttime hunter. It can catch mice in complete darkness! The discs of feathers around this owl's eyes help direct sound waves to its ears.

This owl doesn't make its own nest. It uses nests made by other birds, like magpie or crow nests.

Northern Saw-whet Owl

This small bird was named after one of its calls. It sounds like a saw being sharpened.

Q: Where do owls go to buy clothes for their babies?
A: To the owlet malls!

The male Northern Saw-whet Owl weighs about as much as an American Robin. The female is slightly larger.

When the female lays her eggs, she stays in the nest cavity, and the male brings her food. She lays an egg every 2 days and can lay up to 7 eggs.

This owl grows into its adult plumage when it is one year old. Until then, the owl has a brown head, cinnamon-colored breast and a white V above its beak.

Lewis's Woodpecker

The Lewis's Woodpecker is one of the largest woodpeckers in North America.

This woodpecker keeps a clean nest. When nestlings poop, the poop is wrapped in a thin skin. The parent uses its bill to grab the bag of poop (called a fecal sac) and carries it away from the nest.

The Lewis's Woodpecker catches flying insects for food. It also eats nuts and berries. In autumn, it hides nuts and insects in tree crevices to store them for winter.

Q: What do you call a woodpecker in the winter?
A: B-r-r-r-d!

Hairy Woodpecker

The **Hairy Woodpecker** eats bugs that crawl on or under bark. Sometimes when it drums, it listens for sound changes to locate insect tunnels in a tree.

Woodpeckers drum trees about 12,000 times per day! A woodpecker doesn't hurt its head when it is drumming because it has a thick, flexible skull to help protect its brain.

The Hairy Woodpecker has a long tongue! Its tongue is at least twice the length of its bill. This woodpecker also has barbs on its tongue and sticky saliva to help it catch bugs.

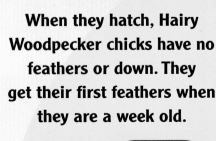

When they hatch, Hairy Woodpecker chicks have no feathers or down. They get their first feathers when they are a week old.

47

Pileated Woodpecker

Pileated Woodpeckers keep insect pests under control. Some of their favorite bugs to eat are carpenter ants, termites and wood-boring beetles that can do a lot of damage to trees.

Large drill holes are signs that a Pileated Woodpecker has been close by. Some drill holes can be longer than a school ruler!

At two weeks old, nestlings will wait at the nest entrance for their parents to feed them. After they leave the nest, the young birds follow their parents around for a few months until they can take care of themselves.

Pileated Woodpeckers make their own nest cavities. Their abandoned nests are used by many other species, like some ducks and owls.

Merlin

The Merlin hunts other birds, so it needs to be a really fast flyer. Its average flight speed is about as fast as a car is allowed to drive in a city (30 mph, 50 km/h)!

A single Merlin can eat more than 700 birds per year! Sometimes a pair will work as a team to hunt a flock of birds.

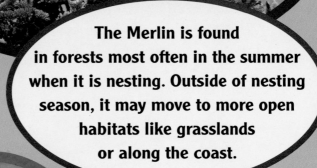

The Merlin is found in forests most often in the summer when it is nesting. Outside of nesting season, it may move to more open habitats like grasslands or along the coast.

In Medieval Europe, people called falconers used Merlins to hunt Skylarks for entertainment.

Steller's Jay

The Steller's Jay is a great mimic. This bird can imitate many sounds, including cats, dogs, chickens, other birds and even telephones!

This jay eats insects, nuts and fruit. In the summer, it hides nuts and acorns in the ground or in trees. It uses its excellent memory to find the hidden food in winter.

Steller's Jay nests are stuck together with mud. They often build their nests in the tops of evergreen trees close to the trunk.

Young birds beg loudly for food and leave the nest after 2½ weeks.

Common Raven

The **Common Raven** is as smart as a chimpanzee or a dolphin, and as good at problem solving as a 4-year-old child! This smart bird likes to play catch, slide down slopes and play tug of war with other ravens!

Q: Why did the raven stand on the telephone pole?
A: He wanted to make a long-distance caw.

The Common Raven uses its strong bill to hammer or rip objects, hull seeds, pry things apart and carry things.

When they hatch, Common Raven nestlings have big bills, thin gray down and almost no feathers. In the early days they can't see. Their eyes don't open until they are 12 days old.

Violet-green Swallow

Violet-green Swallows catch flying insects in mid-air. They often gather together in small groups while feeding. Being in groups may help them to keep a lookout for predators.

A group of these birds is called a gulp or a richness of swallows.

Nestlings grow quickly. When they hatch, they weigh one-tenth as much as their parents, but when they are 12 days old, they weigh more! By 27 days old, when they leave the nest, the young swallows have lost the extra weight and weigh as much as their parents.

57

Chestnut-backed Chickadee

The **Chestnut-backed Chickadee** is the smallest chickadee in North America. It is named after its *chickadee-dee-dee* call and its richly colored back.

Spiders and caterpillars are its favorite foods, but it eats many different insects and seeds.

The female lays her eggs on a soft mattress of moss and fur. When she has to leave the nest, she covers the eggs with a thin blanket of fur!

This chickadee is often seen hanging upside down on tree branches. It looks for food in the lower part of the tree and works its way toward the top.

59

Bushtit

Bushtits are rarely found alone. They often travel in groups of 4 to 60 birds, communicating with twitters and chirps. In winter they huddle together to keep warm.

Q: What do you call two birds in love? A: Tweethearts!

Bushtits eat many kinds of small insects. They need to eat most of their body weight in insects every day!

The Bushtit builds a long sock-like nest that can be the same length as a ruler. Other adult birds sometimes help a mating pair build the nest and feed the nestlings.

61

White-breasted Nuthatch

The White-breasted Nuthatch is usually seen in deciduous forests. It is also known as the upside-down bird because it often walks along tree trunks head down.

When it moves head-first down trees, a nuthatch can't use its tail for support like other birds do. It relies on its strong feet to grip the bark.

The White-breasted Nuthatch will often smear insects around its nest to keep predators away.

This bird wedges seeds or nuts into cracks in tree bark. The bird then hammers the nuts with its bill to hatch them open. This is why is it called a nuthatch.

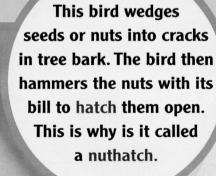

Brown Creeper

The Brown Creeper blends in well with the tree trunks it climbs. It could easily be mistaken for a piece of bark until you see it move!

When a Brown Creeper feels threatened, it spreads its wings against the tree trunk and freezes. It hopes it won't be seen, and it is probably right!

This bird makes its nest behind a loose piece of tree bark.

The Brown Creeper uses its long, curved claws to spiral its way up trees looking for insects. In winter it also eats seeds. A group of Brown Creepers is called a spiral of creepers.

House Wren

The male House Wren loudly sings his cheerful, bubbly song in spring and summer. In the morning he may sing 600 songs or more in a single hour!

The House Wren brings spider egg sacs into its nest. When they hatch, the spiders eat mites that live in the nest and bother the wren.

This bird eats insects, which are hard to find as summer ends. So this wren migrates to the southern U.S. or Mexico for the fall and winter where there are still plenty of insects.

Early hatching House Wrens have an advantage. Nestlings that hatch last grow more slowly and are smaller as adults than nestlings that hatch first!

Blue-gray Gnatcatcher

Though it is called a gnatcatcher, this bird doesn't eat many gnats. It usually eats spiders, caterpillars, wasps and flies. Its constantly moving tail may help to disturb insects.

The Blue-gray Gnatcatcher has earned the nickname Little Mockingbird. It often mimics other birds' calls and its coloring is similar to the larger Northern Mockingbird.

The Blue-gray Gnatcatcher's nest is made of plant fibres and lichen. It is held together with sticky spider webbing or caterpillar silk.

The Blue-Gray Gnatcatcher sometimes raises Brown-headed Cowbird chicks. The cowbird lays its eggs in other birds' nests instead of raising its own young. The cowbird chicks quickly grow to be even bigger than adult gnatcatchers!

Golden-crowned Kinglet

The Golden-crowned Kinglet eats small insects that it picks off leaves and branches.

Q: What's a bird's favorite tv show?
A: The feather forecast!

The female's crown is only yellow.

The male Golden-crowned Kinglet has an orange and yellow crown. He displays his flaming orange crown when he is excited or fighting with other birds.

A group of these birds is called a dynasty or a castle of kinglets.

Western Bluebird

The Western Bluebird doesn't have blue feathers! It is just a trick of the light. The bird's feathers absorb all light wavelengths except blue. The blue wavelengths reflect off the feathers, making them look blue!

Q: What do you call a sad bird?
A: A bluebird!

The Western Bluebird needs to eat about 8 caterpillars or 77 grasshoppers per day to survive.

The Western Bluebird may nest more than once in a breeding season. The second nest is often built on top of the first one!

Males that have no mate may help a breeding pair defend their nest and feed the nestlings.

Swainson's Thrush

This bird's plumage helps it blend into a background of tree trunks and fallen leaves. It is often heard before it is seen.

Along the Pacific Coast, the Swainson's Thrush has more rusty-colored upperparts. In other parts of North America, its upperparts are more grayish or olive in color.

The Swainson's Thrush has song duels to defend its territory. The songs get louder and higher in pitch as opponents try to out sing each other.

The Swainson's Thrush eats mostly insects in spring and summer, and berries in fall and winter. In the fall it migrates to Central and South America.

Gray Catbird

The Gray Catbird is named for its cat-like *mew* call. It is also a skilled mimic and can imitate at least 44 species of birds! Also, it has a special throat structure so it can sing with two voices at the same tIme!

The Gray Catbird eats insects and fruit. In the winter, most of its diet is fruit, but in the spring when more insects are available, it eats mostly insects.

The female Gray Catbird incubates her eggs for about two weeks. When the eggs hatch, she pecks at the eggs and removes the shell to help free the nestlings.

Gray Catbird eggs are bright blue!

Cedar Waxwing

This bird got its name because of the red waxy-looking tips on its flight feathers. The color comes from the berries the bird eats.

Cedar Waxwings travel in large flocks, often gathering together in a single tree. A group of waxwings is called a museum or an earful of waxwings.

For the first two days of their lives, nestlings are fed mostly insects. From three days old onward they get more fruit in their diet.

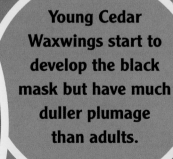

Young Cedar Waxwings start to develop the black mask but have much duller plumage than adults.

Red Crossbill

The Red Crossbill's bill is made for getting seeds out of conifer cones. The shape of a bird's bill depends on what types of trees are in its habitat.

Even though this bird is named the Red Crossbill, only the male is red. The female is yellow.

The Red Crossbill holds a conifer cone with its foot while it uses its bill to pry open the scales. It removes the seed with its tongue, starting at the bottom of the cone and spiraling upward.

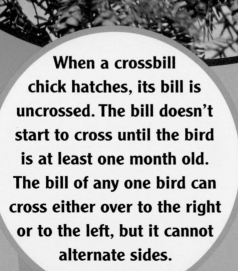

When a crossbill chick hatches, its bill is uncrossed. The bill doesn't start to cross until the bird is at least one month old. The bill of any one bird can cross either over to the right or to the left, but it cannot alternate sides.

Pine Siskin

The Pine Siskin
is a social bird.
In the winter, it gathers in
large flocks, and in the
summer it nests in colonies.
Breeding pairs may
even visit each other's
nests once the eggs
have hatched.

The Pine Siskin eats sunflower and thistle seeds. It clings to the flower head and dines on the seeds inside. This bird also eats insects, and it loves salt! Sometimes it can be seen on highways licking road salt.

The Pine Siskin has a thin bill that is perfect for reaching into thistles to get the seeds.

Chipping Sparrow

The Chipping Sparrow is named after its sharp *chip* call. Outside of the breeding season it may gather in large tournaments (flocks) of more than 200 birds!

The Chipping Sparrow eats mostly seeds, but in the spring and summer it will also eat insects like caterpillars, butterflies, beetles and grasshoppers.

This sparrow makes its nest in conifer trees.

When the young are 5 days old, they have big appetites! Parents return to the nest about every 5 minutes to feed them.

Song Sparrow

The Song Sparrow has 24 subspecies across North America. They all look slightly different!

Q: How does a bird with a broken wing manage to land safely?
A: With a sparrowchute!

The male Song Sparrow sings his cheery, rhythmic song to mark his territory and to attract a mate. Males with fancier songs are more successful at attracting a female.

The Song Sparrow tucks its bill into its back to sleep. It sleeps standing up on a branch or in a crack in a rock.

Bullock's Oriole

The body of the male Bullock's Oriole is an orangey golden color, while the female has a yellowish golden head.

Q: How do orioles stay fit?
A: Worm-ups!

This bird eats mostly caterpillars and fruit, but it dines on other insects, too. When it preys on bees, it is smart enough to pull off the stinger before eating the rest of the bee!

The female Bullock's Oriole weaves her hanging nest out of grass, wool, hair and bark strips. It can take her up to two weeks to build the nest!

Yellow-rumped Warbler

The Yellow-rumped Warbler has two main forms, the Audubon's, which has a yellow throat, and the Myrtle, which has a white throat. The yellow-throated Audubon's is more common in the West.

Q: What do you call a bird that can't walk straight? A: A warbler!

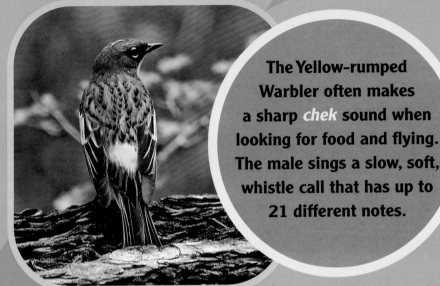

The Yellow-rumped Warbler often makes a sharp *chek* sound when looking for food and flying. The male sings a slow, soft, whistle call that has up to 21 different notes.

A warbler drinks water by filling its bill and then tilting its head back to swallow. Birds can get a lot of their water from their food, but birds this size usually need to drink at least twice a day.

Western Tanager

The Western Tanager gets its red color by eating insects that have eaten a certain type of conifer buds!

The Western Tanager spends its time in the upper branches of trees. It usually looks for food and builds its nests at about 5 metres (16.5 feet) above the ground, about as high as a second-floor window.

This bird eats many types of insects, and sometimes fruit. Wasps are one of its favorite foods!

Black-headed Grosbeak

In some songbirds, only males sing. For the Black-headed Grosbeak, both males and females sing. The female's song is usually a simpler version of the male's song.

This grosbeak's large bill makes it easy for the bird to crack open hard seeds and eat hard-bodied insects.

Monarch butterflies are poisonous to most animals. The Black-headed Grosbeak is one of the few birds that can eat them without getting sick.

© 2020 KidsWorld Books
Printed in China

All rights reserved. No part of this work covered by the copyrights hereon may be reproduced or used in any form or by any means—graphic, electronic or mechanical—without the prior written permission of the publishers, except for reviewers, who may quote brief passages. Any request for photocopying, recording, taping or storage on information retrieval systems of any part of this work shall be directed in writing to the publisher.

The Publisher: KidsWorld Books

Library and Archives Canada Cataloguing in Publication

Title: Forest birds of the West / Genevieve Einstein & Einstein Sisters.
Names: Einstein, Genevieve, 1977– author. | Einstein Sisters, author.
Identifiers: Canadiana (print) 20200403117 | Canadiana (ebook) 2020040315X | ISBN 9781988183268
    (softcover) | ISBN 9781988183275 (EPUB)
Subjects: LCSH: Forest birds—Identification—Juvenile literature. | LCSH: Forest birds—Juvenile literature. |
LCGFT: Field guides.
Classification: LCC QL677.79.F67 E46 2021 | DDC j598.173—dc23

Photo credits: Front cover: GettyImages: iculizard. *Back cover:* GettyImages: Harry Collins; kahj19; elementals.

Bird Illustrations: Gary Ross, Ted Nordhagen, Ewa Pluciennik, Horst Krause

Image Credits: From GettyImages: Aarinahabich, 36; ArmanWerthPhotography, 90; Astrobobo, 55a; BirdImages, 95b; Bob Hilscher, 25a; Brent_1-western form, 15; BrianEKushner, 12a, 24b, 28a, 34b, 65b, 76b; ca2hill, 40; cadifor, 50b; CampPhoto, 53; Carlos Marin, 10b; Carol Hamilton, 27b, 47b; ChezBriand, 61; Christiane Godin, 48a; creighton359, 16a; Cris Ritchie Photo, 87a; Dee Carpenter Photography, 75b; Derwyn, 26b; Devonyu, 56a; Diane Exner, 39a; EdwardSnow, 73b; elementals, 9a; Fireglo2, 52a; fusaromike, 44, 45; GreenSprocket, 18a; Harry Collins, 49ab; ImagesByMJ, 29a; JAH, 41a; jamesvancouver, 8a; Janet Griffin-Scott, 18b, 19b; Jeffengeloutdoors.com, 14a; Jim Williams, 78b; JLRDesign, 79b; JMrocek, 41b; JoanBudai, 72; JohnPitcher, 51b; Jukka Jantunen, 21ab; Jupiterimages, 25b, 79a; kahj19, 80; Kateryna Mashkevych, 10a; KGrif, 14b; LagunaticPhoto, 35b; Larry Dallaire, 16b; Leon Gin, 84b; lissart, 11a; LorraineHudgins,78a; Lynn_Bystrom, 8b; M. Leonard Photography, 30b; MarvVandehey, 35a; mav888, 52b; McBenjamen, 23a; Megan Lorenz, 42a; Milan Krasula, 54; milehightraveler, 93b; mirceax, 27a, 63b; mooninwell, 73a; Motionshooter, 91b; mtruchon, 26a; OldFulica, 60; PamSchodt, 69b; PaulReevesPhotography, 13a, 24a, 58, 66ab, 71a; Peter Senyi, 11b; photographybyJHWilliams, 43a, 89b, 91a, 92; psahota, 13b; randimal, 12b, 37b; RCKeller, 23b, 84a; Rejean Bedard, 34a; robert brown, 76a; Robert Winkler, 48b; SandyTambone, 68a; scooperdigital, 50a; skiserge1, 37a; spates, 56b; StephM2506, 28; SteveByland, 47a, 67b, 77a, 82, 95a; suefeldberg, 46ab, 62; tntphototravis, 31; Vassiliy Vishnevskiy, 55b; Wildpix645, 89a; zhuclear, 19a, 59b. *From Flickr:* Andrey Gulivanov, 32ab, 33ab; Alan Schmierer, 30a; Andy Reago and Chrissy McClaren, 81; Becky Matsubara, 67a, 86, 88; Brandon Trentler, 20a; Bureau of Land Management, 38a; Caitlin Ceci, NPS, 22a; Christian Fritschi, 9b; Darren Kirby, 59a; Deborah Freeman, 29b, 74; Dennis Murphy, 85; devra, 64b; Don Faulkner, 83b; Don Henise, 65a; Elizabeth Nicodemus, 42b; gailhampshire, 38b; Gregory _Slobirdr_ Smith, 61; Hans Norelius, 75a; Jamie Li, NPS, 22b; Joshua Mayer, 44; Bettina Arrigoni, 93a; Larry Lamsa, 83a; N. Lewis, NPS, 70, 71b; Neal Herbert, Yellowstone NP, 17a; NechakoRiver, 57; Nick Varvel, 94; Paul Hurtado, 20b; Sam May, 43b; Shawn Taylor, 63a, 68b, 69a; the real Kam75, 17b; Tracie Hall, 87b; Zia Fukuda, Bureau of Land Management, 39b. *From Wikimedia Commons:* Jeff the quiet, 77b; Melissa McMasters, 64a.

Icons: GettyImages: Alexander_Kizilov; ChoochartSansong, rashadashurov, MerggyR, agrino, lioputra, FORGEM, Stevy, Intpro, MaksimYremenko, Oceloti, Thomas Lydell, Sudowoodo.

We acknowledge the financial support of the Government of Canada.
Nous reconnaissons l'appui financier du gouvernement du Canada.

Funded by the Government of Canada
Financé par le gouvernement du Canada | Canadä

PC: 38-1